Introduction to Mythology for Kids

INTRODUCTION TO
MYTHOLOGY
FOR KIDS

LEGENDARY STORIES
FROM AROUND THE WORLD

ZACHARY HAMBY

ILLUSTRATED BY KAILEY WHITMAN

ROCKRIDGE
PRESS

For general information on our other products and services or to obtain technical support, please contact our Customer Care Department within the United States at (866) 744-2665, or outside the United States at (510) 253-0500.

Rockridge Press publishes its books in a variety of electronic and print formats. Some content that appears in print may not be available in electronic books, and vice versa.

Interior and Cover Designer: Julie Gueraseva
Art Producer: Tom Hood
Editor: Laura Bryn Sisson
Production Editor: Rachel Taenzler
Illustration © Kailey Whitman, 2020
Author photo courtesy of © Rachel Hamby

ISBN: Print 978-1-64739-320-5 | eBook 978-1-64739-321-2
R0

For Opal, Onyx, and Baby John

"Since it is so likely that they [children] will meet cruel enemies, let them at least have heard of brave knights and heroic courage. Otherwise you are making their destiny not brighter but darker."
—C. S. LEWIS

"When we lose our myths
we lose our place in the universe."
—MADELEINE L'ENGLE

CONTENTS

INTRODUCTION

Myths are full of wonders—things you don't see
in everyday life like magic, beasts, and monsters.
Myths were first told by people who wondered why
the world works the way it does. Why does the sun
shine more in the summer? Why does the wind
blow? Why does it sometimes not rain enough?
Myths helped explain the mysteries of life for whole
groups of people. These stories were told over and
over for many hundreds of years. Along the way,
some of the deeper meanings were lost. Different
versions of the same story emerged. But myths still
fill us with wonder.

Myths also have lessons to teach. The heroes of myths go on adventures, and along the way, they learn lessons about right and wrong (sometimes the hard way). As you journey along with them, you can learn the same lessons.

Although the myths in this book come from all around the world, look for similarities within them. Since myths show a group of people's hopes, dreams, and fears, these similarities show us that maybe people are not as different as we might think. Enjoy the wonder!

MOMOTARŌ
THE PEACH BOY
Japanese

In ancient Japan, there lived a poor old man and woman who had no children. One day, when the old man had gone to gather sticks and the old woman had gone to the stream to wash their clothes, she noticed something strange—and orange—bobbing its way down the stream. It was an enormous peach.

"That peach would make quite a feast!" she cried. But the peach was too far out and began to float on by. Just then, the old woman remembered a song she had learned long ago. She spoke the words,

"Far waters are bitter, but near waters are sweeter. Pass the bitter, and for a treat, come into the sweet." The peach seemed to hear her words and floated into shore. She laughed as she carried the peach all the way back to her house. When the old man arrived home and saw the giant peach, he licked his lips and brought out his knife to cut into the peach's soft skin. But before he could, little giggles filled the air, and the peach skin opened like the petals of a flower. In the middle, where normally there would be a pit, sat a smiling baby boy.

"We cannot eat this!" cried the old man in shock.

"Don't you see, husband? This baby is a gift! A son for us in our old age!" So the old couple named their special boy Momotarō, which means "peach boy."

Momotarō grew up to be stronger, faster, and smarter than all the other boys in the village. His parents told him that he was meant to do great things since he had been born from a peach.

One day when he was fifteen, Momotarō overheard his parents discussing some terrible news. People all across the countryside had been stolen away by horrible horned monsters called **Oni** and trapped on their cursed island. Without hesitation, Momotarō spoke, "I must go and save these poor people." Although his parents begged him not to go, he replied, "I am born of a peach! I will do great things!" The old woman had no sword to give her son, but gave him a bag of freshly made **dumplings** for his long voyage.

Momotarō set out on his journey, traveling down the road that led to the sea. He had no idea how he would defeat the Oni with no weapon to protect himself. As he munched on his mother's tasty dumplings, a snarling dog stepped into his path. "Peace, friend," Momotarō said, tossing the dog a dumpling. "I am going to the island of the Oni. Will you come with me?" Tasting the wonderful dumpling, the dog fell in step behind him.

"I'd follow you to the ends of the earth for another dumpling, Lord Momotarō!"

Soon after this, they heard a chattering. A monkey appeared in the overhead branches. "Peace, friend," said Momotarō, throwing the monkey a dumpling. "Will you come with me to Oni Island?" The monkey's little face lit up with glee.

"For this I'd follow you anywhere, Lord Momotarō!"

Finally, a pheasant landed on the pathway, crying its bird cry. Momotarō gave it a dumpling and an invitation. "Mmmm. Lord Momotarō, I will serve you forever!" the pheasant said.

Pressing on, Momotarō and his animal friends reached the sea, where across the waves they could see the shadowy island of the Oni. "Before we sail across," Momotarō said, "we should eat more dumplings to give us strength." When they later reached the island fortress, they saw that it was swarming with Oni of all different shapes and colors. All of the monsters had terrifying horns and roared like a storm at sea.

Momotarō confronted them bravely. "Foul Oni, I have come to defeat you once and for all!"

When the Oni saw only a boy and three animals, they roared with laughter. But their smiles quickly faded. The dog ran forward and bit at their ankles. The monkey pelted them with rocks. The pheasant pecked at their tender heads. Momotarō picked them up and hurled them to the ground. At last, the Oni cried for mercy. "Spare us, mighty warriors!"

"I will only spare you if you agree to break off your horns," declared Momotarō. So the Oni broke off their horns and vowed to do no more harm the rest of their days. They freed their prisoners and gave Momotarō all of their magical treasures. The boy returned home to his parents with armloads of treasure and his animal companions at his side. And everything was simply peachy.

GILGAMESH AND ENKIDU

Mesopotamian

Long ago in **Mesopotamia,** there was a golden city called Uruk. It had the highest walls and the tallest **ziggurat** the world had ever seen. The city's king was a young man named Gilgamesh, who some people said was part god. Gilgamesh definitely looked like a god—he was handsome and tall. He was also a deadly archer and a powerful wrestler, but there was one thing he was not: a hero. Gilgamesh did not treat his people kindly. In fact, every citizen in his beautiful city lived in fear of him. All the young men who lived there were forced to fight in his wars or build his buildings to even greater heights. All the young women were taken away to live in his palace.

Finally, the subjects of Gilgamesh had had enough. They prayed that someone mightier would come and teach him how to rule his people fairly. But where would anyone find a man mightier than Gilgamesh?

The gods saw what Gilgamesh was doing to his people, and they were not pleased. Yet no creature mightier than Gilgamesh existed on the earth. So they decided to create a new one. One of the gods pinched off a bit of clay and let it fall to the earth. The clay became Enkidu, a man whose body was covered in thick fur. Enkidu had the mind of a man but also the strength of an animal. Only then could he be strong enough to defeat Gilgamesh.

But Enkidu was more interested in running through the woods and living like a wild creature. So the gods sent a wise woman to tame him. She cut away his fur, dressed him in regal clothes, and taught him how to speak like a human. When she was finished, he looked just like a prince! Then she told him his mission: He must go to Uruk to challenge the selfish king Gilgamesh.

At first, Enkidu did not want to leave the wilderness to battle a man he had never met. But when the wise woman named all the ways that Gilgamesh hurt his own people, Enkidu became angry. "No man should treat others in such a way!" said Enkidu. "I must teach him a lesson!"

So Enkidu traveled to the golden city of Uruk and called for Gilgamesh to meet him face-to-face. News reached Gilgamesh that a beast-like man was seeking him, so he went down from his ziggurat to meet with Enkidu. At first glance, the two gigantic men could tell they were nearly equals in strength and power. "Speak quickly, whoever or whatever you are," said Gilgamesh.

"King Gilgamesh, I come from the gods with a message for you," Enkidu said. "You must not mistreat your people."

Gilgamesh was not used to being told what to do. "How dare you!" snarled Gilgamesh. "I will not be told what to do by some beast!"

But Enkidu replied wisely, "Who is more beastlike? I, who look like a beast? Or you, a man who acts like one?"

Gilgamesh roared and rushed at Enkidu, and the two fought fiercely. There had never been a wrestling match like it before. Their struggle knocked down walls, destroyed buildings, and shook the entire earth! Finally, Gilgamesh realized that Enkidu was the only creature in the world that he could not beat. For the first time in his life, his great strength was not enough. "Fine!" he cried. "I will yield to you!"

Exhausted from their great struggle, the two mighty men sat breathlessly upon the ground.

"I cannot believe it," said Gilgamesh. "No one has ever matched me."

"Will you listen to my message now?" asked Enkidu. "You must be kind and fair to your people. Stop being greedy and selfish!"

"But that is all I know," said Gilgamesh. "My whole life I've lived only to please myself."

"Then I will show you," said Enkidu kindly. That day, King Gilgamesh, who thought he had it all, gained something new: a friend. He and Enkidu had many more adventures. They traveled to the ends of the earth defeating all kinds of monsters, and their friendship grew and grew. Along the way, Gilgamesh became a hero to his people. He learned to rule them with respect and wisdom. Enkidu had made Gilgamesh into a better person—as friends are meant to do.

VASILISA THE WISE

◆ Slavic ◆

There once was a girl named Vasilisa, who had a loving father and mother. Then her mother became ill, and she called Vasilisa to her bedside. "Take this doll," her mother said. "It will help you when I no longer can." A few days later, Vasilisa's mother died, and all Vasilisa had left of her was the plain-looking doll.

Soon after, Vasilisa's father married again. His new wife was a woman with a beautiful face but a heart as cold as an empty fireplace. She did not like Vasilisa and searched for a way to be rid of her. One day, when Vasilisa's father was away, her stepmother cried out, "Oh dear! The fire has gone out! Vasilisa, there is an old woman who lives in the deep woods. Go borrow some fire from her!"

As Vasilisa stepped out of her cottage door into the dark forest, she thought she heard a small voice say, "Vasilisa, do not be afraid." She looked down in shock at the doll she clutched in her hands. Had it spoken? "Your stepmother is sending you to the house of Baba Yaga, the terrifying witch of the deep wood who eats children. But if you listen to me, I will protect you. Before you leave, take a bit of bacon, a few rolls, and some oil for your journey." So she did.

The stepmother smiled as Vasilisa disappeared into the forest, thinking she had gotten rid of her forever. The woods grew deeper and darker around Vasilisa. Soon, she reached what could only be the home of Baba Yaga. It was a strange cottage surrounded by a fence made of bones. The cottage itself stood on two chicken legs. It was alive and bewitched by magic. Whenever someone approached the cottage, it would turn away, so no one could come inside.

"Don't worry about the cottage," said Vasilisa's doll. "I know the words to make it keep still." So Vasilisa spoke the secret command to the cottage. It squawked like a chicken, lowered to the ground, and allowed Vasilisa to enter.

As Vasilisa's eyes adjusted to the darkness, she saw Baba Yaga sitting in the middle of her cottage, grinning a gruesome grin. The witch's enormous nose almost touched her chin. "I have come to borrow a bit of fire," said Vasilisa.

Baba Yaga looked at her fireplace, which glowed with blue flame. Then she cackled. "Doomed child, you will feel my fire soon enough! I must fly away for a bit of business. When I return at nightfall, I will cook you up!" Baba Yaga then climbed inside her mixing bowl, which was the size of a bathtub. "Make sure she does not escape!" she shouted to her cat. Then, using a large stirring stick as an oar, Baba

Yaga pushed the bowl into the air and whooshed out of the cottage.

"All is not lost," the doll whispered to Vasilisa. "Give the bacon to the cat." Vasilisa did, and the cat eagerly ate it up.

Then the cat bowed to her and spoke, "Sweet girl, I am in your debt. Collect a bit of that blue fire in a pot and escape while Baba Yaga is away. Take this comb with you, and throw it behind you if she follows you." Vasilisa took the fire and the comb. She thanked the cat and headed out of the cottage.

"You'll need the rolls now," the doll told her. As soon as Vasilisa stepped foot into the yard, a pack of fearsome dogs ran around the cottage, barking and biting. But when Vasilisa threw the rolls down, they snapped them up and let her pass in peace.

Vasilisa then made her way to the yard gate, but when she reached to open the gate, it cried out, "The child is escaping!"

"Put the oil on the gate's hinge," the doll whispered. So Vasilisa did, and the gate stopped its crying. The doll said, "Now, hurry home! Night is falling!"

At dusk, Baba Yaga returned in her flying mixing bowl, only to find her cottage empty. She yelled at the cat, the dogs, and the gate. "You scum! Why did you help her escape?"

"She was nicer to us than you ever were!" they all replied.

Meanwhile, Vasilisa ran through the dark forest. Behind her, she heard the witch growing near in her flying bowl, so she threw down the comb that the cat had given her. The teeth of the comb became a row of enormous trees that Baba Yaga could not fly through. Vasilisa heard Baba Yaga cursing her through the tangled branches, but she dared not look back.

When Vasilisa's stepmother saw her return home alive, she could not believe it. "Show her the fire," the doll said. When Vasilisa held up the blue fire, it caused her stepmother to disappear in a puff of smoke. "Serves her right," said the doll. And so Vasilisa lived happily ever after with her father and her enchanted doll.

ANANSI
AND THE SKY
GOD'S STORIES

—◇— West African —◇—

Anansi looked like a man, but he looked like a spider, too. In fact, he had extra arms and legs and could spin webs. He lived on the earth among human beings, and he was always watching for ways his clever tricks could make their lives better.

Anansi saw that the humans seemed sad. They had nothing to make their lives happy and bright.

Then he remembered that in the palace of Nyame the Sky God there were magical things called *stories*. These things could make anyone happy. The Sky God owned all the stories in the world. In fact, there were piles and piles of them all over the sky palace—and plenty enough to share.

"That's it! Humans must have stories!" So Anansi spun his web up into the sky and climbed up, up, up into the heavens. He climbed so high that the human villages were tiny dots below him. Then, at last, he arrived at the Sky God's palace.

Nyame greeted Anansi from his throne. "Anansi, have you come to hear another one of my stories?"

"The lives of the humans are so dreary. They need something to give them hope. I was thinking you might share your stories with them," Anansi said.

"You expect me to *share*?" the Sky God said, laughing.

"Do you need so many?" Anansi asked. "Could you not spare a few?"

The Sky God did not want to share his precious stories, but he also did not want to appear selfish. So he settled back into his throne and folded his hands. "Fine, Anansi. I will share my stories with the human beings . . . only after you complete four tasks for me." Then the Sky God named the four most impossible tasks anyone could ever imagine: "You must capture Mmoboro the deadly **hornet** swarm, Onini the killer **python**, Osebo the stealthy **leopard**, and Mmoatia the mischievous fairy."

Nyame expected Anansi to give up right then and there, but instead Anansi said, "Very well. Human beings will have your stories soon, and they will tell most of them about me!"

Anansi lowered himself back down to earth. The tasks that the Sky God had given Anansi were challenging, but he had a secret weapon: his wise wife. Anansi went to Aso, his wife, and told her of the tasks placed before him. "Hmmm. Those are difficult tasks," she said. "Luckily you have me to help you!" They talked it over and devised a solution to each of the challenges.

First, Anansi set out to find Mmoboro, the deadly hornet swarm. Along the way, he made a hole in a gourd and filled it with water. Then he plucked himself a banana leaf. He found the hornets buzzing angrily around their nest. Anansi approached them, shielding his head with the leaf, and pouring the water over himself.

"Hurry, friends! The rains are coming! Hide in this gourd until the rain passes!" Hornets hate the rain more than anything, so they swarmed into the gourd, and Anansi quickly plugged the hole. He jiggled the gourd a bit and chuckled to himself. "One down!"

Next, Anansi had to trap Onini, the killer python. Anansi knew he was very vain. When Anansi found the great snake curled up on a rock, Anansi called out, "Greetings, friend! I came to settle an argument. My wife says you aren't the longest creature in the world."

"Ha! No creature is longer than me," hissed the python.

"I believe you, but my wife does not." Anansi said, "Let me measure you, and this will prove it!" So he had the python stretch himself out on a long stick. "This is no good! You keep curling up at the ends! I guess I must tie you." He tied the python's head and tail down to the stick to keep him from curling. "Look at that! I guess you *are* the longest creature," said Anansi. "But now you are trapped! Two down!"

Then Anansi went in search of Osebo the stealthy leopard that has teeth as sharp as spears and can walk without even rustling the grass. "He will sneak up on me and kill me," said Anansi, "unless I trap *him* first." So Anansi dug a pit in the ground and covered it with leaves, and then he sat down nearby and waited. Sure enough, Osebo the leopard came creeping silently along and was ready to spring on Anansi. But Osebo's next step was a step too far, and he fell down into Anansi's pit.

"Anansi," cried the leopard. "You ambushed me!"

Anansi smiled and said, "I only did what you were planning to do to me!" Then he covered the leopard with his spider webbing and hoisted him out of the pit. "Three down," Anansi chuckled to himself.

Finally, Anansi had to trap Mmoatia, the mischievous fairy, whose magic was even greater than his. But he knew how to outwit her. Anansi crafted a beautiful little doll, just the same size as the fairy, and covered it all over with sticky **sap**. In the doll's lap he placed a delicious dish made from mashed **yams**. It did not take long for the fairy to appear, lured by the smell of the dish.

"Oooh, little girl. May I have some of those yams?" the greedy fairy asked. The doll did not reply, so the fairy grew angry and slapped it on the cheek. The fairy's hand immediately stuck to the sap on the doll's cheek.

"Let go!" the fairy shrieked. Then the fairy slapped the doll with her other hand, which also stuck. She kicked and clawed and bit at the doll until she was completely trapped by the sap.

Anansi walked up and said with a laugh, "Four down!"

Anansi returned to the Sky God with his captives—the trapped hornets, the tied-up python, the webbed leopard, and the sticky fairy. The Sky God was not pleased, for he knew he must give up his beloved stories. But a bargain is a bargain. "Very well. Take these stories to the earth. Give them to humans. They will be eternally grateful to you. In fact, they will call all great tales 'spider stories' from this day forward because of you."

Anansi bowed low to the ground and said, "Thank you, my lord. I can think of no greater gift than that."

It all came true—just as the Sky God had said. To this day, it is hard to experience the joy of a story without thinking of Anansi and the great gift he gave all humankind.

FINN MacCOOL FACES A GIANT

Celtic

Whenever Finn MacCool found himself in trouble, he would suck his thumb. Don't get the wrong idea. He wasn't a baby. He was a grown man—a huge man, in fact. He was a great hero of Ireland. Then why did he suck his thumb? Once when he was just a boy, Finn helped his old teacher catch a fish called the Salmon of Knowledge. Whoever ate of the fish would gain all sorts of secret wisdom. Finn's teacher instructed him to cook it up, but not to eat any of it. Finn obeyed the order, but as the fish cooked, he accidentally burned his thumb and quickly stuck it into his mouth. In doing so, he tasted a bit of the magical salmon. All kinds of knowledge flooded into his mind. From then on, all Finn had to do was suck his thumb, and a bit of that knowledge would come back to him.

Finn grew up to be bigger and stronger than other men. He used his strength to defeat all kinds of monsters and evil spirits. Eventually, he decided there was no one in the whole world that could ever defeat him. That's when Finn heard about Benandonner the giant. Folks said that Benandonner was even more powerful than Finn MacCool. Finn couldn't believe it. "I am the mightiest man who ever lived! I must meet this so-called giant and whittle him down to size!"

Finn had a beautiful and smart wife named Oonagh. Hearing her husband's boast, she sighed. "Dear, is it wise to pick a fight with a man you have never seen?" asked Oonagh.

"Ha! I will fight Benandonner and win!" replied Finn.

Word of Finn's challenge spread. The news reached all the way to Scotland, where Benandonner lived, but all the giant did was laugh at Finn's threat. "Who is this tiny Irishman who thinks he can beat me?"

When Finn heard the giant's response, it was too much for him to bear. There was no bridge across the sea between Ireland and Scotland, so he ripped boulders up from the ground and made a stepping-stone path across the water. "Watch out, Benandonner! Here I come!"

Finn crossed his self-made bridge, his heart leaping at the thought of victory. Yet when he reached Scotland, his heart leapt for a different reason: He caught sight of Benandonner, who was even bigger than folks had said. Ten times as large as Finn at least! Finn ran home across his bridge as quickly as he could.

His wife smiled to herself when she saw Finn returning. "Back so soon, dear?"

"Oonagh! You have to save me!" Finn cried in fright. "There's no way I can beat Benandonner. And I've made a pathway that he can cross to kill me!"

Although she truly wanted to say, "I told you so," instead Oonagh said, "Do exactly as I tell you, and I can save your life."

Later that same day, Benandonner made his way across the sea using the boulder pathway Finn had made. The giant lumbered right up to the door of Finn MacCool's house. His footsteps nearly shook off the roof, but Oonagh answered the door calmly. "Yes? May I help you?"

"Is Finn MacCool here?" the giant asked. "I've come to defeat him."

"No, he is away," Oonagh said. "But please come in and wait for him."

The giant barely managed to squeeze into the house. Inside, there was no sight of the mighty Irish hero. Oonagh stood beside a cradle that snuggled a baby, which was really Finn in disguise. "This is my child—the son of Finn," Oonagh said.

"That is a big baby!" Benandonner said.

"Oh, yes! Someday, he will grow twenty times that size and be as big as his father."

"Twenty times?" Benandonner asked, looking suddenly nervous.

"Oh, where are my manners?" Oonagh said. "Here. Have a pancake while you wait." Oonagh had baked several iron griddles into the pancake she offered up to the giant. When he bit into it, a few of his teeth fell to the floor.

"Argh! My teeth!"

"Oh my!" Oonagh cried. "These pancakes are Finn's favorite! He chews them so easily. Look! Even baby Finn can eat them." She fed a regular pancake to the baby, and he gulped it right down. "I'm sorry! I had no idea you were so weak."

"Weak? Weak?" roared Benandonner. "I will crush your puny husband in my mighty grip!"

"Mighty grip, huh?" said Oonagh slyly. "Can you squeeze water from a stone? My husband does that all the time." She held up a white stone.

"That's impossible!" snapped Benandonner. He grabbed the white stone and squeezed and grunted and strained, but he could not make water come from it. "See! It's impossible!"

"Oh, really?" said Oonagh. She handed another stone to the baby. Or at least that is what it looked like. She had actually put a large, white cheese **curd** into Finn's grip, and he squeezed for all he was worth. Milky water gushed out of the curd.

Looking more frightened than ever, Benandonner moved to take a closer look at the child.

"He is a strong lad for one so young. And cute, too!" The giant scratched Finn's chin with an enormous finger. "Gootchie-goo!"

Now Finn had been sucking his thumb this entire time (as part of the act), and a bit of knowledge came to him. He realized that Benandonner had a magic finger, which was the source of almost all his strength. Finn raised his head and bit the giant's finger for all he was worth.

"Ahhh-eeeee!" cried the giant. "My finger! Let go! Let go!"

Benandonner nearly tore the house apart trying to free himself, but Finn held on. Finally, he burst free and fled back toward Scotland as quickly as he could. He never wanted to meet the hero Finn Mac-Cool face-to-face. His baby son had been bad enough.

Finn and Oonagh watched the giant disappear over the horizon. "Will you be picking any more fights with giants?" Oonagh asked.

"No, I have learned my lesson," replied Finn with a smile.

Benandonner had reached the sea. Too frightened to even look over his shoulder, he destroyed the boulder pathway as he ran across, ripping up the stepping stones. The scattered stones left behind are still known today as the **Giant's Causeway**. They are a constant reminder not to pick fights lightly.

THOR AND LOKI IN THE LAND OF THE GIANTS

Norse

Thor the thunder god pounded his strong fist on the wooden door before him. Loki the trickster god stood at his side, looking frightened. "Do we have to be here?" he asked nervously.

"We do," said Thor, shaking his enchanted hammer, which he always carried with him. "I want to teach these giants a lesson! I want to teach them to stop playing tricks!" Thor was the sworn enemy of the frost giants. They were constantly playing all kinds of evil tricks on him and the other gods of **Asgard**.

Now Thor and Loki were standing at the door of the castle of the Giant King. The door was so tall that they could barely see the top of it.

"But they're smarter than we are!" said Loki. "That's why they're so good at tricks!"

"Ha! Smarts!" Thor said with a laugh. "Their smartness is useless against my strength! I am Thor!"

Just then, the door was answered. It swung open to reveal a room full of hideous, humongous giants, all glaring at Thor and Loki. The Giant King looked down from his throne with a cruel grin.

"Thor, the enemy of the giants!" the Giant King said. "Have you come to challenge us?"

"I have!" said Thor, walking bravely forward. "I have come to show you once and for all that we gods are better than you giants. Suggest any test, and I will beat you at it!"

"Very well," the Giant King said. "If you are really as strong as you say, then you will have no problem winning a wrestling match."

"I can beat any opponent!" bragged Thor.

"Good," said the Giant King. "Then you will have no problem defeating . . . my grandmother."

As Thor stared in shock, an old woman, ancient and hunched over, hobbled forward.

Loki laughed. "Go easy on Granny, Thor."

Thor couldn't believe it, but he shrugged. "A challenge is a challenge." He rushed forward to wrestle the old woman to the ground. To his surprise, he found that she was quite strong. They wrestled for ten minutes. She went down on one knee, but Thor could not force her to the ground. Meanwhile, the giants howled with laughter.

"Enough! You cannot win. Granny is too strong for you!" said the Giant King. "Now for your next opponent: the greatest monster in all the land . . . my cat!"

An enormous, fluffy cat came forward and plopped down on the floor.

"All you have to do is lift it," the Giant King said, smirking.

Thor ran forward and struggled against the cat. After several minutes he managed to lift its belly, but the cat arched its back and kept its paws firmly on the floor. The giants were wiping tears of laughter from their eyes. Even Loki was chuckling.

"Ha! Enough! You lose again," the Giant King said. "Maybe a drinking contest would be better. All you have to do is finish this drink!"

A **drinking horn** filled with **mead** was given to Thor. The god began quickly gulping it down. But no matter how much he drank, the mead inside never grew less. Thor kept gulping. His face turned red, then blue, then purple. Finally, he spewed mead in all directions and fell to the floor. The giants fell down too, for they were laughing so hard.

"I . . . I . . . I don't understand," Thor murmured.

"Thor, you have been beaten today, but take heart," the Giant King said. "We beat you only through magic. You were tricked! The old grandmother you wrestled was actually Old Age. No living thing can beat her. But you forced her down to one knee. No one has ever done so much. And what you thought was my cat was actually the Midgard Serpent, a snake so large it surrounds the entire world. You managed to lift it out of the ocean where it lives. And speaking of the ocean, the drinking horn we gave you was magically connected to the ocean itself. You managed to lower the ocean by a few inches before you were defeated."

"Cheaters!" roared Thor. He did not like to lose. He ran forward with his hammer raised, ready to clobber them all to death. But still laughing, they all disappeared—the Giant King, his subjects, and the castle itself.

Only Loki was left, grinning at Thor. "Let's go home," said Loki. "It looks like you learned the lesson today. Brains are mightier than muscles."

MAUI
SLOWS THE SUN
Polynesian

Maui, the great hero and clever trickster, was always fixing things for the people of earth. First, he had fixed the sky. It had hung down too low, and the people of earth were always bumping their heads on it. So he lifted it up where it belonged. Problem solved.

Then Maui saw that there wasn't much land for the people to live on, and the ocean went on and on. So he went fishing. He lowered his magical fish-hook into the water and instead of catching fish, he caught whole islands, pulling them to the ocean's surface one by one.

But there was still one problem that Maui had not solved: the sun.

The sun appeared spectacularly every morning in his flowing, red robe, shining his glorious light over the earth. But as soon as he had risen, he would hitch up his robe and run across the sky as swiftly as his long legs could carry him. Before the people on earth knew it, the sun was across the sky, his light was fading, and they were left in darkness.

Life was hard for the people with dusk and dawn only a small time apart. There simply wasn't enough time to work or play before the light of the sun was gone for the day. Maui saw this, and it angered him. Even his beloved mother, Hina-of-the-Sun, could not finish her **tapa** cloth, which she made from dried bark. There was never enough sunlight to dry it out.

Maui raged to his mother, "It's the sun's job to give light to the world, but he doesn't take his job seriously! Someone should slow him down!"

Maui's mother knew he would not rest until he had done just that, so she sent him to talk to his grandmother, who lived on the slopes of a great mountain, which was the House of the Sun.

When Maui's grandmother saw him coming, she asked, "What are you planning to fix about the world now, Maui?"

Maui smiled. "I'm going to slow down the sun!"

Maui's grandmother gave him the instructions he needed. In order to slow the sun, he would need to weave long, strong ropes from coconut fibers. At the end of the ropes he would need some hair from his sister, Hina-of-the-Sea, to make nooses that would trap the sun.

"The sun won't give up without a fight," added Maui's grandmother. "So you'll also need this stone axe." She held it out to Maui.

Maui worked hard, weaving his coconut-fiber ropes and tying nooses onto their ends. With his ropes completed, Maui climbed to the top of the mountain. It was actually a hollow volcano, and the sun lived inside. Maui carefully laid out the ropes and the nooses around the volcano's opening. His plan was to catch the individual rays of the sun in the nooses. And that is exactly what happened.

The sun began to rise. First came the sun's golden rays, which were caught in the nooses one by one. Maui pulled the ropes tight and anchored them to the ground. Then, finally, the sun himself rose in all his glory. Expecting to soar into the sky, he realized that he was tied down to the mountaintop!

"Who dares?" the sun yelled, his blazing anger flashing out. "Who dares to challenge me?"

"I do," said Maui, stepping forward.

"Ha! Maui!" the sun scoffed. "Do you think you can fix *me* now?"

"Yes," said Maui calmly. "You are not taking your responsibility seriously! The people of earth need your warmth and light. You must run more slowly across the sky."

"I am the sun! I take orders from no one!" The anger of the sun blazed out, and the heat began to burn up the ropes that held him. Before this could happen, Maui ran forward and struck at the sun with the stone axe.

"Ouch! Stop!" cried the sun, who cared deeply about his appearance. "Don't ruin my beauty!"

Maui lowered his axe and said, "I will spare you. But you must think of others and travel more slowly."

The sun pouted. "If I run quickly, I can come back home sooner and sleep much longer. I need my beauty rest, you know."

"Fine," said Maui. "We will make a deal. For half of the year, you will agree to travel the skies more slowly. Then, for the other half of the year, you can travel as quickly as you wish."

"Agreed," said the sun. "Now free me from these ropes!"

So even to this day, for half of the year the sun stays in the sky longer, and for the other half the sun passes over quickly. When there is enough daylight to work and play, the people of earth know they have Maui to thank for it.

GLUSCABI AND THE WIND EAGLE

Abenaki, Native Northeastern United States and Canada

In the beginning, when Tabaldak the Owner had finished making human beings, he dusted off his hands, and some of the dust fell down upon the earth. From the pile of dust, a creature crawled out.

"Who are you? Where did you come from?" asked the Owner. "I did not create you."

"I am Gluscabi," said the creature. "And I created myself from this leftover dust here."

The Owner looked at Gluscabi closely. "You are different from my creations, but you are wonderful."

So Gluscabi came into being. He was not as powerful as the Owner, but he possessed some of his power to change things. And he did change things—sometimes not for the best.

Since Gluscabi was so different from the other humans, they would not accept him. So he went to live among the animals. An old woodchuck took him into her **lodge** to live as her son.

"You can live here, but you must not cause any trouble," said Grandmother Woodchuck. "You have great power, but you must use it for good, not evil."

"Of course, Grandmother," Gluscabi said. Yet Gluscabi could not help himself. He grew impatient with the way the world worked, and sometimes he would use his power to change the things he did not understand.

One day, Gluscabi wanted to go duck hunting, so he paddled his canoe out onto the lake—or at least he tried. The wind was blowing so hard that it pushed his canoe right back to the shore. *Whoosh!* He tried to row out a second time, but once again the wind was too strong. *Whoosh!* Throwing his paddle to the ground in anger, Gluscabi stormed back home.

"Grandmother, tell me—where does the wind come from?" Gluscabi asked. Grandmother Woodchuck could tell he was angry.

"Oh, Gluscabi, I do not like it when you ask questions like that," said Grandmother Woodchuck. "It always brings trouble."

"If you do not tell me," said Gluscabi, "I will find out for myself."

"I will not withhold wisdom from you," said Grandmother Woodchuck. "The wind comes from the flapping wings of Grandfather Wuchowsen, the wind eagle, who lives high in the mountains."

"That is all I need to know. Thank you, Grandmother." Gluscabi left the lodge without saying another word and began to climb into the mountains. "The wind has ruined my plans for the last time," he muttered to himself.

As he climbed higher and higher, he could tell he was getting closer because the wind grew stronger and stronger. He continued to climb. The wind blew so hard that it blew off his shoes. *Whoosh!* He continued to climb. The wind blew so hard that it blew off his clothes. *Whoosh!* He continued to climb. The wind blew so hard that it blew the hair off his head! *Whoosh!* Then, when he had nothing else for the wind to blow off, he reached the mountain peak where Grandfather Wuchowsen was perched, flapping his wings for all he was worth.

"Grandfather!" cried Gluscabi over the roaring wind. "Stop!"

The eagle stopped and looked at the naked, bald creature before him. "Who—or what—are you?"

"I am Gluscabi. I came to tell you what a wonderful job you are doing making the wind," said Gluscabi slyly.

"Why, thank you!" said Grandfather Wuchowsen. "Nothing is mightier than the breeze I make with my powerful wings!"

"True! But listen to this," Gluscabi said, "I know of a mountain peak far from here that is even higher than this one. Perched on it, you could make the wind blow even harder."

"Really?" the wind eagle asked. "I don't know if such a thing is possible, but please show me at once!"

"You have worked your wings so hard today," Gluscabi said. "Why don't you let me carry you there?"

"Oh, you are very kind," replied the wind eagle.

"But, you know, it will be much easier for me to carry you if your wings were at your side," Gluscabi said thoughtfully. "Here. I will tie them for you." Grandfather Wuchowsen allowed Gluscabi to bind his wings. Once Gluscabi had the eagle bound, he lifted him over his head, but instead of carrying him down the mountain, he pitched him into a nearby **ravine**.

"Hey!" the eagle cried. "What are you doing? You can't leave me in here!"

Then Gluscabi dusted off his hands. "That takes care of the wind! Back to duck hunting!"

Gluscabi returned down the mountain and paddled out onto the lake in his canoe. It was much easier without the wind blowing. But something had changed. It was hotter now. There was no breeze to cool him off. The lake waters were growing foamy without the wind to stir them. And there were no ducks to be seen.

Gluscabi went home to Grandmother Woodchuck.

"Gluscabi, what have you done?" she asked. "The wind stopped suddenly, and the air is hot and still!" Then Gluscabi told Grandmother Woodchuck all that he had done.

"Oh, Gluscabi. Don't you see? The Owner put the wind eagle on the mountain for a reason. The wind cools the air. It blows clouds down the mountain to bring us fresh rain. The breeze keeps the waters clean. We need the wind."

"I understand, Grandmother," said Gluscabi. So he climbed back up to the mountain peak and freed Grandfather Wuchowsen, who was still in the ravine where Gluscabi had left him.

As Gluscabi returned the wind eagle to his peak, he apologized. "I am sorry, Grandfather. I see why you must do what you do. Yet let me speak a bit of wisdom to you that I have learned: Sometimes it is good for the wind to blow. And sometimes it is good for it to be still."

Grandfather Wuchowsen nodded his head in understanding. Then Gluscabi went down the mountain wiser to the ways of the world.

Even to this day, sometimes the wind blows, and sometimes it is still.

THE DRAGON'S PEARL

Chinese

Once there was a boy and his aging mother, who lived in a village near the Min River. Times had grown hard. The rain had stopped falling, and the mighty Min River became shallow. The villagers whispered that the River Dragon had lost his power to send the rains. For, you see, dragons have mighty powers that control the forces of nature. Soon many of the villagers were starving.

To feed himself and his mother, the boy had to cut grass and sell it in exchange for a tiny bit of rice. As the drought got worse, the boy had to go farther and farther from his home in search of any green grass. Then one day, after walking farther than ever before, he discovered a patch of the tallest, greenest grass he had ever seen. He cut it at once and returned to his mother. "Mother, look at this! I must return to that spot again tomorrow!" He did return and found that the same patch of green grass had regrown in the night. "Impossible!" said the boy, but it was so. Day after day, he returned to the same spot and harvested the lush grass, which they sold for rice.

Although the boy and his mother now had plenty to eat, it was such a long way to walk every day. So the boy's mother made a suggestion. "My son, dig up the patch of grass and replant it here. Then you will not have to go so far every day."

The son thought this was a good idea, so he walked to where the grassy patch was and began to dig in the ground. As soon as he did, he uncovered a shining, white pearl in the soil. He ran all the way home leaping for joy! Now he and his mother would be wealthy!

"This is good fortune!" said his mother, and she hid the pearl at once in the family's rice jar. "But we must not let anyone see!"

The next day, when the boy returned to the patch of tall grass, it was withered and brown. It seemed the miracle had ended. The boy returned home heartbroken, but his mother called out to him as he entered their house.

"Look! Look!" She pointed to their rice jar, now overflowing with rice. "This must be a magic pearl!" she said. "It made the grass grow, and now it makes the rice increase." So they put it into their money box, which had been empty for so long. The next morning, the box was overflowing with coins.

"Do you know what this means?" the boy said. "Our village is saved!"

The kind mother and son used the magic of the pearl to increase their wealth and food, and they shared this prosperity with the other villagers. Soon, everyone in the village had plenty to eat and plenty of money in their money boxes.

But some people in the village wanted this fortune for themselves. These wicked neighbors spied on the mother and son in their hut and saw them using the magic pearl. They beat on the door and shouted, "You have been hiding a treasure from us! Hand it over!"

"We must not let them find the pearl!" cried the mother.

The mob was about to break in, so the boy slipped the pearl into his mouth to hide it. But as he did, his mouth and throat burned with thirst. "Water! Water!" he cried, running out of the house and down to the river, with his mother following behind him. The river was low from the drought, but the boy fell on his knees and began to guzzle up what water was left. As his mother watched in shock, he drank the whole river!

Then his eyes became golden, his body lengthened, his skin turned to brilliant scales, and his head grew beautiful horns. He had transformed into a mighty dragon.

"I see now!" cried his mother. "The magic pearl once belonged to the River Dragon. He lost it, and you found it!"

The boy-turned-dragon opened his mouth, and water flowed out again, filling the river to the brim for the first time in many years. Then he turned to dive into the water. His mother tried to hold him back, crying, "No, my son! Don't go!" The boy looked back at her one last time before he vanished into the river forever.

As his mother sat crying on the riverbank, she said, "My son, you have stopped the drought caused by the dragon's lost pearl. But now you must take the dragon's place. You must watch over us and make sure there is always plenty."

The great dragon, deep in the river, heard his mother and did exactly as she said.

THE SEARCH FOR THE MAGIC LAKE

Incan

In spite of his wondrous wealth, the great emperor of the Incas was heartbroken. His only son had fallen ill, and no doctor in the entire empire could heal him. The emperor knew his son would soon die unless a miracle happened. Then one night as he prayed, a golden **flask** appeared in the ashes of the fire before him. A voice spoke in his ear: "At the end of the world is a magical lake whose waters will heal your son."

The emperor wasted no time. He grabbed up the golden flask and sent a message throughout his empire: "Whoever brings back water from the magic lake at the end of the world will be rich beyond measure!"

Many heroes tried to find the magic lake, but they all failed. People began to doubt that the lake existed at all. The emperor's son grew closer and closer to death. This is when two brothers played a very foolish trick. They lied to the emperor and claimed to have gathered water from the magical lake. When the water did not heal the sick child, the emperor had the two brothers thrown in prison.

Now the father and mother of these two brothers were heartbroken. They were poor farmers—too old to work the farm themselves—and their sons were in prison. Their only other child was their little daughter, Sisa. "Don't give up!" Sisa told her parents. "Let *me* go and find this magic lake! I can heal the emperor's son, free my brothers, and win us a fortune! There's always a way." Her parents did not want her to go. She was only a little girl, after all. But her parents realized they had no other choice.

Sisa took her family's only llama with her as she set out on her journey. "Do you know how to find the end of the world?" Sisa asked her llama, but it did not answer. "Hmmm. I will just have to trust that there is a way."

They journeyed into the high country, where the mountain peaks seemed to touch the sky. But days passed, and there was no sign of the magic lake. It seemed that Sisa's quest would end in failure.

One day, as Sisa rested, she heard **macaws** chirping in the tree overhead. She was about to eat the last bit of crushed corn she had brought for her journey, but instead she spread it out for the birds. "Share my meal," she said. The birds swooped down to peck at the food. "Do you know how to find the end of the world?" she asked.

To her shock, the birds answered, "We do." Each of the macaws lifted up its wing and plucked a single feather from its side. "Use these feathers," the birds said. "Form them into a fan. When you are holding this fan, simply imagine where you wish to be, and our feathers will carry you there. The fan will also protect you from the monster that guards the lake."

So Sisa took up the feathers and made them into a fan. Then, after hugging her llama friend goodbye, she imagined herself standing on the edge of the magic lake. She felt the wind lifting her and heard the macaws calling out, "Farewell!" When Sisa lowered the feather fan, she was standing on the edge of an enormous lake, where the mountains and the sky become one.

Then Sisa heard something roaring above her. A winged serpent with scales as red as blood swooped down from the sky toward her. She quickly covered her face with the fan. The serpent stopped. Its eyes closed, its wings stopped flapping, and it fell to the ground asleep.

"The fan did protect me!" Sisa cried. "Now for the magic water!" It was only when she knelt by the water's edge that she realized she had no way to carry it. Then she saw a golden flask lying in the mud at the lake's edge. She used this to scoop up the magical water. Placing the fan before her face again, she imagined herself standing in front of the emperor. The next thing she knew, she was there.

The emperor jumped in shock to see a young girl appearing before him. Sisa held out the golden flask and said, "Here! This will heal your son!"

The emperor recognized the flask as the same one that had appeared to him many years before. He took the water to his son, who was healed by just one sip. "I cannot believe it! A little girl has saved my son and my kingdom!"

In return for Sisa's bravery, the emperor freed Sisa's brothers from prison and presented her family with a large farm and a herd of llamas to tend. Generation after generation of emperors drank magical water from the golden flask, and they all enjoyed good health. And it was all because of little Sisa, who found a way.

PHAETHON
AND THE CHARIOT OF THE SUN

— Greek —

Phaethon was a boy in ancient Greece. He was teased constantly by the other boys his age, because he did not have a father. So one day he asked his mother, "Who is my father? Or do I even have one?" Then she told Phaethon a secret: He did have a father—a powerful one—who lived so far away and was so busy that Phaethon had never seen him before. Phaethon's father was Helios, the sun god himself.

"Every day he drives his shining **chariot** across the sky," Phaethon's mother told him. "That is why he cannot be with us. If he did not do his job, there would be no light to shine upon the world!"

Phaethon proudly told this news to the other boys, but they only laughed at him. They did not believe that the sun god was truly his father.

"Fine!" Phaethon said. "I will prove it to you!"

Far on the eastern edge of the world lay the Palace of the Sun. That is where the sun begins its journey every morning. Phaethon knew that is where he would find his father, and he set out on a journey. He walked for days and days, and finally he reached the magnificent, shining Palace of the Sun. The golden doors of the palace were decorated with all the patterns of the stars in the heavens.

Phaethon knocked upon the doors, and he was ushered into the magnificent palace. Inside he saw the Days, the Hours, and the Years all lined up—waiting for their time to pass. And at the end of the palace hallway, he saw his father seated on a shining throne.

Helios removed his glowing crown and looked upon the face of his son for the first time. "My son! You're here! But why have you come so far?"

"To meet you, Father," Phaethon said. "And now that I am here, I want to ask you a favor."

"You are my son, and I love you," Helios said happily. "I will promise you whatever you wish! I swear it by the **River Styx**."

"Let me drive your golden chariot," said Phaethon. "If my friends see me driving it, they will realize that I am truly your son."

"Oh no, Son," said Helios. "That is far too dangerous!"

"You don't understand," said Phaethon. "They tease me and mock me!"

"Then they are not truly your friends. You have nothing to prove to them. Take my advice—not my chariot. The sky path is so steep that I can barely navigate it myself. There are animal-like

constellations in the sky that will attack you. I barely escape from them day after day."

Although Helios pleaded and pleaded, Phaethon would not listen. But his father could not say no. When a god swears on the River Styx, he cannot break his promise.

As Dawn was nearing, Phaethon excitedly climbed into his father's chariot. Helios shed tears as he smeared protective **ointment** on Phaethon's body and placed the glowing crown on his son's head. "Please, Son! I do not want to lose you so soon after meeting you!"

"It will be fine!" said Phaethon with a careless shrug.

Dawn threw open the palace doors, and Phaethon whipped the fiery horses into motion. The chariot roared up into the sky, and Phaethon quickly realized that he could not control the horses. The steeds ran wild, taking the sun far off course.

Fearsome animals with starry bodies lunged out of the sky, trying to gobble up Phaethon as he flew by. The chariot flew too high and bumped the sky. Then it swooped too low, scorching the land and causing the oceans to boil and even dry up.

"Wait! Please! I've learned my lesson! I no longer want to drive the chariot!" cried Phaethon. But it was too late.

The gods on **Mount Olympus** saw that the earth would be destroyed if something was not done. Reluctantly, Zeus, the lord of the gods, took aim at Phaethon's chariot with one of his thunderbolts. With a lightning strike of power, the chariot was destroyed. Phaethon fell to earth, flickering like a falling star, and was never seen again. Because of his carelessness, the earth now has places that are dry and scorched as well as those that are green and growing.

ISIS AND OSIRIS

Egyptian

The god Osiris was a powerful and wise king of Egypt. With his sister, Isis, at his side, he taught his people how to grow wheat and barley to make bread and how to make laws and live in peace. Because of these things, he was much loved by the Egyptian people.

But Set, the dog-faced brother of Isis and Osiris, was jealous and secretly hated Osiris. Set wanted the throne for himself. So he hatched a plan to end his brother's kingship as soon as it began. Late one night, Set snuck into Osiris's bedroom and measured him from head to toe while he slept. The plot was in place.

Set hosted a special celebration where he showed all the gods a marvelous, rectangle-shaped box covered in sparkling jewels. Then Set announced, "Whoever of you can fit perfectly inside this box shall be its new owner." Many of the gods and goddesses climbed into the box, but they were all too tall or too short. Finally, it was Osiris's turn. When Osiris lay down in the box, it fit him perfectly.

As the other gods watched in shock, Set slammed the box lid shut and sealed up the cracks so that it was airtight, killing his brother. Osiris's box had become a **coffin**. Set placed the coffin in the **Nile River** and laughed as it floated away. Then he named himself king.

All of this happened while Isis was far away, or she would have been able to save her brother. When she heard of Osiris's death, she rushed to the river in search of the box. She had to find his body and perform the proper rituals, so his spirit could pass into the **land of the dead** and be at peace.

Disguised as a **mortal** woman, she went among the men and women of earth, hoping to hear any rumor of what had happened to her brother's body. After years and years of searching, she heard a story about a magical tree—one that was enormous, with the most beautiful, **fragrant** blooms. Isis knew that such magic must have come from the gods. She was right. Osiris's coffin had floated down the Nile and washed up onto the roots of the tree. The tree had quickly grown around the coffin, trapping it inside.

The magical tree was in Byblos, the oldest city in the world. Isis sailed to Byblos at once, but once there she learned surprising news: The tree had been cut down and made into a **pillar** of the king and queen's palace.

Isis went to the palace and appeared before the king and queen. She demonstrated her magic to them and then asked them to break open the pillar that had been crafted from the magical tree. The king and queen were shocked when they found the golden coffin within.

Isis thanked and blessed the king and queen of Byblos, loaded the golden coffin onto her boat, and sailed back toward Egypt. Little did Isis know that Set had sent his evil spies out to follow her. Howling with rage, Set rushed out to catch her.

When Isis finally reached Egypt, she had Osiris's golden coffin unloaded onto the riverbank. She planned to perform the funeral rituals as soon as possible. But she was too exhausted from her journey and soon fell asleep.

Set arrived when night fell. At the sight of Isis asleep beside the coffin of Osiris, he chuckled to himself. Set's hatred was so powerful that he did not even want his brother to find peace in the land of the dead. Set removed the body of his brother from the coffin and ripped it to pieces. Then he flung the pieces far across the world. Now there was no hope of Osiris making it to the land of the dead.

When Isis awoke and saw what Set had done, she thought her heart would break. All her work had been for nothing. But the **jackal**-headed god, Anubis, came to her aid. Anubis was the god of the underworld. He was also the protector of the newly dead. He embalmed their bodies so they wouldn't decay and could pass into the afterlife. As she and Anubis found each piece of Osiris's body, the body parts were preserved in the form of a mummy.

When the final piece of Osiris was found, an amazing thing happened. The spirit of Osiris rose and told Isis not to be sad. Though his spirit must pass into the land of the dead, a new ruler would come to protect the people of Egypt. Isis would give birth to a son, Horus, who would defeat the evil Set.

Osiris bowed and thanked Isis for her devotion. He then went forth into the underworld, where he would become the king of the dead. As Osiris's spirit faded away, Isis knew her journey was over. Her faithfulness had saved her brother's soul.

GLOSSARY

Asgard: The home of the Norse gods

chariot: A two-wheeled carriage pulled by horses

coffin: A box in which a dead body is placed

constellation: An arrangement of stars

curd: An almost-solid glob of curdled milk

drinking horn: A cup made from an animal's horn

dumpling: A tasty food made from balls of dough

flask: A drink container

fragrant: Having a sweet or pleasant smell

Giant's Causeway: A rocky path-like outcrop on the coast of Northern Ireland

hornet: A large wasp with a painful sting

jackal: A type of wild dog found in Africa and southern Asia

land of the dead: An underground world where the ancient Egyptians believed the spirits of the dead resided

leopard: A large, spotted, cat-like predator

lodge: A type of Native American dwelling place

macaw: A colorful parrot most common in Central and South America

mead: A drink made from honey, common in ancient times

Mesopotamia: An ancient civilization in the modern country of Iraq

mortal: Not having the ability to live forever; the opposite of immortal

Mount Olympus: The mountain on which the ancient Greeks believed the gods lived

Nile River: A long river that flows through Egypt

ointment: An oily paste used on the skin as medicine

Oni: Japanese monsters who have brightly colored skin and frightening horns

pillar: A vertical support that holds up a building

python: An enormous snake that squeezes its victims to death

ravine: A deep and narrow opening in the ground

River Styx: A river that the ancient Greeks believed flowed through the underworld, the land of the dead

sap: A sticky substance that flows through trees

tapa: A cloth made from dry bark

yam: A tasty root vegetable, like a potato, that is common in Africa

ziggurat: A rectangular, stair-stepped tower in ancient Mesopotamia

RESOURCES

Want to learn more about myths from around the world? Here are some great books to check out.

D'Aulaires' Book of Greek Myths, by Ingrid and Edgar D'Aulaire (Delacorte Books for Young Readers, 1992).

D'Aulaires' Book of Norse Myths, by Ingrid and Edgar D'Aulaire (New York Review Books, 2005).

Favorite Folktales from around the World, by Jane Yolen (Pantheon, 1988).

The Hero's Guidebook: Creating Your Own Hero's Journey, by Zachary Hamby (Creative English Teacher Press, 2019).

Myths of the Norsemen, by Roger Lancelyn Green (Puffin Books, 2013).

Native American Stories, by Michael J. Caduto and Joseph Bruchac (Fulcrum Publishing, 1991).

Tales of Ancient Egypt, by Roger Lancelyn Green (Puffin Books, 1967).

Tales of Greek Heroes, by Roger Lancelyn Green (Puffin Books, 2009).

REFERENCES

Caduto, Michael J., and Joseph Bruchac. *Keepers of the Earth: Native American Stories and Environmental Activities for Children*. Golden, CO: Fulcrum Publishing, 1997.

Cole, Joanna. *Best-Loved Folktales of the World*. New York: Anchor Books, 1983.

Doyle, Malachy. *Finn MacCool and the Giant's Causeway*. New York: Hachette Children's Group, 2015.

Green, Roger Lancelyn. *Tales of Ancient Egypt*. London: Puffin Books, 1967.

Hamilton, Edith. *Mythology*. New York: Grand Central Publishing, 2011.

Lin, Te. *Teach Yourself Chinese Myths*. New York: McGraw-Hill, 2001.

Rosenberg, Donna. *World Mythology*. New York: McGraw-Hill Education, 1994.

The Epic of Gilgamesh. Translated by Andrew
George. London: Penguin Books, 2003.

Yolen, Jane. *Favorite Folktales from around the World.*
New York: Pantheon, 1988.

ABOUT THE AUTHOR

Zachary Hamby is an English teacher in rural Missouri. Being a lifelong fan of myth and legend, he loves teaching young people about heroes, both ancient and modern. He has written and illustrated the Reaching Olympus series, the Mythology for Teens series, and *The Hero's Guidebook*. He resides in the Ozarks with his wife, Rachel (who's also an English teacher), and their two children. For more information about Zachary visit his website CreativeEnglishTeacher.com or contact him by email at hambypublishing@gmail.com.

ABOUT THE ILLUSTRATOR

 **Kailey Whitman** has always looked at picture books very closely. When she was small, she had an active imagination and a lot of questions, so she took to making her own pictures and hasn't stopped. She went to school where she majored in making pictures and since then has been making pictures for books, magazines, newspapers, posters, walls, and for everything and anything else she can. When she's not drawing, she's usually enjoying the outdoors, reading, or walking her dog. To see more of Kailey's work, please visit KaileyWhitman.com.

CPSIA information can be obtained
at www.ICGtesting.com
Printed in the USA
JSHW041636051021
19344JS00001BA/2